THE NEIGHBOR-TO-NEIGHBOR JOB CREATION ACT:
[NTN]
Six Months To Full Employment

By

Jim Green

DEDICATED TO:

The OECD—in the hope that their policy makers will read
this and bring our current market economies into the 21st
Century....
Amen

ISBN-13: 978-1500443160

ISBN-10: 1500443166

PROLOGUE

The Neighbor-To-Neighbor Job Creation Act [hereafter
NTN] provides us with the legal mechanism to limit our
unemployment—so that at no time in the future will our
unemployment rate in America exceed 3%. And the
perplexing question asked, here, is why didn't we do this
years ago?

In a thumbnail, it is a federally mandated Social
Insurance, owned by our employed, to provide a fund to
hire/train our unemployed.

And without crossing all the t's, and dotting all the i's—
[the actual proposed legislation—ready to go into the
hopper—is ahead]…the policy cost for this insurance

would be limited to 4% of salary—and yes, if one works in America—from the POTUS on down—they would be required to be a policy holder. It is US, helping out our neighbor...

In picking up on 'why on Earth didn't we do this years ago'—we have had on the books, since 1978 [15 USC § 3101, commonly known as Humphrey-Hawkins], the "legal authorization" to create a "reservoir of public employment" anytime our unemployment rate rises above "3%"....

And to complete the legal mechanism, above, our Social Insurance fund would be triggered anytime our unemployment rate in America, would so rise above 3%....

To put this in context, we have been three times over this percent during far too much of the Great Recession—and we are currently over twice this percent, as I write, as we inch along--year after year, in a sluggish recovery, i.e., the inevitable result of the path we are currently on—and without getting too cyncial—with one foot still on the plantation [more on this shortly].....

And while, so it seems, the mind automatically defaults to: This is about a liberal social safety net---NTN is, in fact, a Pro-Market concept—and a critical next step in our capitalist economic evolution, i.e., NTN is *Indispensable* to the *Effective* functioning of our 21st Century market economy...and it won't add a dime to our deficit.....

Also, in fairness regarding our dragging our feet in implementation—we do have a lone Congressman, Conyers who periodically introduces legislation to enforce the "legal authorization" in Humphrey-Hawkins, HR 870 and currently HR 1000—to name two—but the black-hearted radical Republicans who currently dominate the House [and also shooting themselves in the foot], will not allow these Bills out of Committee....

And it cannot be stressed strongly enough: This is a Pro-Market concept, based on pragmatism....I am a capitalist, so please spare dragging out "literal" vs "critical" thinking—too much time has already been wasted on nonsense, i.e., communism, socialism lunacy [and without getting too elitist...better liberal, than literal—with the latter not thinking at all]....

For some background, in 1960, our market-driven economies [currently 34 countries]--around the globe joined together given their common market objectives-- the Organization for Economic Co-operation and Development, and commonly referred to as OECD.

For the most part the OECD got it right on the money in strengthening the market economy concept....regarding unemployment, however, and to this day, they have it dead wrong....they keep looking to the market to do something it is *incapable* of doing.....i.e., create enough jobs......

That is, their policy makers, including the U.S., cling to the belief: "The market can provide anybody wanting a job, with a job"—when, in fact, this has *never* been true— with our Welfare system, alone, in America as empirical evidence Exhibit One....with the result....

"High and persistent unemployment has pervaded almost every OECD country since the mid-1970's.", as reported by internationally recognized Economist, Dr. William F. Mitchell, with double-digit, i.e., 12.6% unemployment common in the Eurozone, and Greece and Spain both in excess of 25%, as I write.....

The major paradigm shift in the world economy in the mid-1970's is explored in detail in the chapters below, but given "automation", alone, NTN, or like programs such as HR 1000, are critical, and indispensable, in solving our joblessness going forward in the 21st Century [Source: Common Sense].....

As reported by ABC News on July 1, 2014 "Eurozone Unemployment Remains High as Economy Lags" .....which is precisely the point of this book, and proposed NTN---

High Unemployment/Sluggish Recovery is not a non-sequitur—people do not buy stuff when they are jobless—It is not smart business—it is anti-capitalism to not fix unemployment—*IMMEDIATELY....yesterday is not soon enough*\

And for a real-time example, here is a truth...Detroit is a ghost town, comparatively....a nightmare, because Washington does not know how to solve our unemployment crisis.....Detroit may be past the point of no return....the jury is still out—but the purpose of this book is to illuminate the path we should be on.....

And it is obvious based on the empirical evidence, alone, that our policy makers in the OECD don't have a clue how to end their/our unemployment crisis.....

A parting thought.....we should never condemn the CEO for closing a plant, when they are losing money....but we should be outraged by policy makers who lack the social/business acumen to address this lapse in a market economy.

In closing out the Prologue, it is transparent that NTN can easily get snarled up in an ideologue sink hole....we humans have a penchant to do that....slap a label on a yet to be employed solution....perhaps, so we don't have to expend any brain power in our evaluation, or for what ever....and even more so in today's pugilistic political climate....

But for absolute clarity---there is _no_ideologue agenda....the _sole purpose_ is pragmatic—is solely about problem-solving—i.e., to address two extremely serious, and inter-locking social problems going forward in the 21st Century.

Unemployment and the resulting damage to our Market economy, as a result.

Closing out with a law I crafted—--for our friends in Economics, in academe:

3% is the zero-sum threshold above which unemployment triggers inflation by diminishing labor training and skills, under-utilizing capital resources, reducing the rate of productivity advance, increasing unit labor costs, and reducing the general supply of goods and services--and the loss in income to the Market is compounded exponentially with each percentage point of increase in unemployment, above 3%.

Short Definition:

3% is the zero-sum threshold above which unemployment starts substantially undermining the Market--and the loss in income to the Market is compounded exponentially with each percentage point of increase in unemployment, above 3%.

Dr. Mitchell closes his daily Blog on Modern Monetary Theory, with "That is enough for today."…and will close out this part of the Prologue with the same, and let the Chapters, below, fill in any blank spots…and agree or disagree, hopefully the offering, here, will have clarity….THX

A few closing comments in the Prologue—As Oscar Wilde averred "The only truly worthless opinion is an unbiased one"—so bias, agreed—but always in the interest in getting at the larger goal—the truth….

Incidentally, I published my first book on my 78th birthday—and not that I write that fast, or well—the materials were all there for the better part of the past 30 years, give or take, gathering dust—it was just a matter of pulling them together in some order—also, don't believe any book should be over 60 pages, plus/minus—i.e., can be read in the crapper--two hours, max--lol—but it seems best summed up by a very astute observer [wish I could recall their name to give credit]. Persons who write do so because they have *no*choice [it is a compulsion, an addiction..]—they become an "author", however, when people start reading what they have written….

Finally, a note to the reader—the papers and letters are not in sequence, and apologize for redundancy [please look for the nuggets...Thx--lol]—also, if you are a "typo-wonk"—are more concerned with sentence structure, etc., than content—you probably won't like my writing—and you will find a wayward capital letter, here and there, and appearing out of place and used for emphasis—I chalk up to editorial license and tongue-in-cheek, self-effacing humor—so apologies, here—[I seriously support: Take what you do seriously, but never yourself....]....

Just look for content, please....THX

CHAPTER ONE

President Obama/Council of Economic Advisers:

As a Delegate to the Texas Democrat Convention this past week, June 26-28, 2014, Dallas, I asked two questions in meetings, in bars, just about anywhere fellow Democrats wanted to jawbone:

1] FULL EMPLOYMENT IS A PRO-MARKET CONCEPT [not coincidentally also the title of a book I have on Amazon—but hang out]....and then I would add [with universal agreement]: Common sense, right—people do not buy stuff when they are jobless, right.....And here is the hammer this setup was leading to:

So why isn't it a fact?

It is our $64,000 question, today, and begs the question [in support of the market, alone] why is it not being asked daily, or hourly in Washington—

We are, in theory, a democracy, so when 86% of Americans believe that "anybody wanting to work should be able to find a job"--EVERY effort should me made to make this a fact—

When, in fact, NO effort is being made in Washington to make this a fact—[lip service, no laws] which raises the additional question are we, in fact, an oligarchy as recent studies suggest? Is this why 50% of Americans don't vote—they don't believe their vote counts?

The other side of this coin is that people not buying stuff undermines the market....our disappearing manufacturing base is not totally due to our jobs going to the Far East....

With the current result a "no one wins"—the jobless lose, and the Market loses…

Which leads to the second question asked of my Compadres:

2] Do you believe the market can provide anybody wanting a job, with a job?

And this is the universal catch-all that undermines our solving the first question asked—We don't look for a solution when we BELIEVE we have one.....

And thus we stand on one foot and then the other waiting on the market to provide our jobs—with the CBO projecting it will be 2017 for us to get back to even an anemic 5.5% jobless rate—and if the market fails in the interim, the jobless are out of luck.....

When the truth is the market has NEVER been able to provide everybody with a job...with our Welfare system empirical Exhibit ONE--And given "automation" alone, going forward—this pernicious BELIEF becomes exponentially less viable, almost daily!

In sum, Humphrey-Hawkins [15 USC § 3101] was ahead of its time—when it was signed into law in 1978, by President Carter—Now it is Indispensable to the Effective functioning of our 21st Century economy—[and implementation via deficit-neutral HR 1000 or The Neighbor-To-Neighbor Job Creation Act, to name two].....

Jim Green, Democrat opponent to Lamar Smith, Congress, 2000

CHAPTER TWO

President Obama/Council of Economic Advisers:

THE HISTORY OF HOW WE GOT WHERE WE ARE

Following WW II, President Truman signed into law the
[FULL] EMPLOYMENT ACT of 1946, to provide
employment for our returning troops.

Ironically, half-way around the world, Australia codified
into their law an almost identical Bill, and for the same
reason—

Difference is—Australia actually put their law into effect,
and over the next 30 years it was intrinsic to employment
policy in Australia that "anybody wanting to work should
be able to find a job"—and save for a brief recession in
1961/62 their unemployment was 2%, or less. This period
is still referred to as their "Golden Age", in Australia.

Unforeseen by either country, however, in the mid-
1970's the world economy underwent a major paradigm

shift as a result of the colliding forces of automation, globalization, technology, etc., reaching a critical mass— in brief, an adjustment towards modernity—From a perverse perspective, we became victims of our success....

The instability caused by this transition, however, resulted in a malaise, and ushered in the ill-winds of greed-driven neo-liberalism with its indifference to unemployment, and the likes of Thatcher and Reagan—and the menace of this greed-driven agenda was exploded by Bush II, resulting in obscene disparities in wealth that persists, and is the cause of much friction between right and left, to this day.

It also ushered in high and pervasive unemployment throughout our market-driven economies, the OECD— with 6% unemployment in Australia now the norm, and double-digit unemployment common throughout the Eurozone, to this day.

As a result of the "malaise", however, the U.S. took an aggressive, pro-active role in addressing the, above, economic shift—and in 1978 President Carter signed into law one of the most important laws in the 20th Century-- an expansion of President Truman's full employment, i.e.,

Pro-Market 15 USC § 3101--which "authorizes" the creation of a "reservoir of public employees" at any time our unemployment in America exceeds "3%"—

But in spite of 3% unemployment being the threshold point above which unemployment starts undermining the Market—

And deficit-neutral HR 870/The Neighbor-To-Neighbor Job Creation Act—A federally mandated Social Insurance, owned by our employed, to provide a fund to hire/train our unemployed—

But in spite of these deficit-neutral, Pro-Market solutions—this Law has never been implemented.

FULL EMPLOYMENT IS A PRO-MARKET CONCEPT, Amazon/Kindle

Jim Green, Democrat opponent to Lamar Smith, Congress, 2000

CHAPTER THREE

Council of Economic Advisers:

PROPOSED LEGISLATION:

THE NEIGHBOR-TO-NEIGHBOR JOB CREATION ACT

A Pro-Market, deficit-neutral, federally mandated, Social Insurance, owned by our employed, to provide a fund to hire/train our unemployed.

SECTION 1. SHORT TITLE.

This Act shall be cited as The Neighbor-To-Neighbor Job Creation Act [To establish employment/training opportunities for the unemployed in compliance with the "Legal Authorization" in Public Law 15 USC § 3101, for the creation of a "reservoir of public employees", anytime our unemployment rate exceeds "3%", with an emphasis on training for market needs, including a training stipend, where there is a shortage of trained workers--hereafter NTN].

SEC. 2. DEFINITIONS.

In this Act the following definitions apply:

(1) SECRETARY- The term `Secretary' means the Secretary of Labor.

(2) STATE- The term `State' has the meaning given such term in section 102(2) of the Housing and Community Development Act (42 U.S.C. 5302(2)).

(3) TRUST FUND- The term `Trust Fund' refers to the Department of Labor Full Employment Trust Fund.

(4) UNIT OF GENERAL LOCAL GOVERNMENT- The term `unit of general local government' has the meaning given such term in section 102(1) of the Housing and Community Development Act (42 U.S.C. 5302(1)).

(5) URBAN COUNTY- The term `urban county' has the meaning given such term in section 102(6) of the Housing and Community Development Act (42 U.S.C. 5302(6)).

(6) WEB SITE- The Secretary shall establish an Internet Web site to serve as an information clearinghouse for job training and employment opportunities funded by the Trust Fund.

SEC. 3. EMPLOYMENT OPPORTUNITY GRANTS TO STATES, LOCAL GOVERNMENT.

(a) Use of Funds–A recipient of a grant under this section shall use the grant primarily for infrastructure repair, including, but not limited to:

(A) The painting and repair of schools, community centers, and libraries.

(B) The restoration and revitalization of abandoned and vacant properties to alleviate blight in distressed and foreclosure–affected areas of a unit of general local government.

(C) The augmentation of staffing in Head Start, child care, and other early childhood education programs to promote school readiness and early literacy.

(D) The renovation and enhancement of maintenance of parks, playgrounds, and other public spaces.

Respectfully Submitted,

Jim Green, Democrat candidate for Congress, Dist 21, TX, 2000

CHAPTER FOUR

President Obama/Council of Economic Advisers:

For several years leading up to the passage of 15 USC §
3101, in 1978, Jessie Jackson and other civil rights
leaders marched annually, on Dr. King's birthday, for
passage of this law—

Specifically, this law has provided us henceforth with the
"Legal Authorization" to limit our unemployment to "3%"
in America…

And then a funny thing happened….the day after it was
signed into law by President Carter, in 1978, we turned
our back on this law, and pretended it didn't exist…i.e.,
zero imagination was expended in putting this "Legal
Authorization" into effect…

That is, in fact, we didn't reduce our unemployment to 3%
[true to this day—our current unemployment rate is more
than twice that, at 6.3%--and in spite of the fact that 86%

of Americans believe that "anybody wanting to work should be able to find a job."]1

And the irony for Carter is that had he, in fact, reduced our unemployment to "3%"…he would have defeated Reagan hands down, in the 1980 election…and America would have been spared the disastrous Republican neo-liberalism policies, since1

And, as just one example—our deficit was a highly manageable $60 billion when Carter handed it over to Reagan, but it was exploded to a staggering $10 trillion by 2008…and it has cost the American people an additional $7 trillion to clean up the mess left by Bush III1

Further, as a DIRECT result of Republican hubris, lies, and policies, our economy went into collapse, twice [in 1987 & 2008]—due to the incompetent and flawed construct of Supply-Side, it has a shelf-life of only 7 years before it sends the economy into meltdown—[and yet, this remains the Republican's One and Only program to this day]1

President Carter/Democrats, however, have not exactly had clean hands in the implementation of this law—and to this day the PROMISE of employment [the market will magically create--a carrot and stick ruse] is used as a SUBSTITUTE for jobs....

In short, the false propaganda that "The market can provide anybody wanting a job, with a job"—is the most pernicious belief in America, today, not only because it is false, the menace it poses to our economy is far more of a danger to the American people, than terrorism....

FULL EMPLOYMENT IS A PRO-MARKET CONCEPT & WINNERS WANT OTHERS TO WIN, Amazon/Kindle

Jim Green, Democrat opponent to Lamar Smith, Congress, 2000

CHAPTER FIVE

President Obama/Council of Economic Advisers:

The Tea Party would fold in a New York Second, if Washington ended our unemployment crisis...pervasive unemployment is the undercurrent in their vitriol and railing against Washington...

The fact is, 86% of Americans believe that "Anybody wanting to work should be able to find get a job"—

But when the mind-set in Washington is to cling to the pernicious and false belief that "The market can provide anybody wanting a job, with a job" [not true since the mid-1970's], the result has been a disaster [the 2010 election which ushered in a House full of lunatics, i.e., Tea Party Republicans], and as well:

5 years after the Great Recession is declared over—we still have almost 25 million unemployed/underemployed—our job creation is moving at a snail's pace, resulting in a sluggish recovery [the

market thrives when we have a robust, employed, consuming workforce], and our job creation is barely able to keep up with our birthrate [and some months falling behind]....

And as well, the CBO projects that it will be 2017 before we return to even an anemic 5.5% unemployment rate—with unemployment benefits long since expired, and if the market fails—the jobless are out of luck!

It is in this milieu, however, and the absence of viable job creation, that demagogues like Ted Cruz can rant endlessly with irrational blather to gin up our unstable and our racists, and create a Tea Party with a lynch mop mentality—

And all the more perplexing since Washington has the "legal authorization", on the books [15 USC § 3101], to reduce our unemployment to "3%", tomorrow.....and particularly given deficit-neutral HR 870....

It is not the lack of jobs, or money—that has caused our unemployment crisis----it is the lack of imagination....

And if this "legal authorization" were enforced—the Tea Party would disappear overnight—vanish—they would cease to be a magnet for our marginalized ...because the impetus for their rage would disappear!

In sum, we are currently on a "no one wins" path—the jobless lose, the American people lose, and the market loses!

See: FULL EMPLOYMENT IS A PRO-MARKET CONCEPT, Amazon/Kindle

Jim Green, Democrat opponent to Lamar Smith, Congress, 2000

CHAPTER SIX

President Obama/Council of Economic Advisers:

The most pernicious *belief* in America, today, is:

The Market can provide anybody wanting a job, with a job.

It is pernicious for two reason:

1] It isn't true—hasn't been true for most of the OECD countries since he mid-1970's—and as a result of automation, alone, it becomes less and less true as we advance in the 21st Century.

2] It drives our job creation policy/law, today, [HR 2847]—and but for this *belief* Republican job creation would be non-existent [Malignant Republicanism speaks of as fact, what, in fact, is wishful thinking--the magic carpet path to job creation].

The corollary to this *belief* is:

Fix the Market, and this in turn will fix unemployment—rather than fix unemployment, and this will fix the Market.

But by our following the former, the CBO projects that it will take until 2017 for us to get back to even an anemic 5.5% unemployment rate, with unemployment benefits long since expired, and if the Market fails—the unemployed are out of luck!

In short, we do not currently have a program *specific* to ending unemployment.

And this, in turn, undermines the Market.

The Market thrives when we have a robust, employed, consuming workforce....

And an expanding and contracting public workforce [for example, the Buffer Stock Employment Model] is an *Indispensable* component to the *Effective* functioning of a modern market economy.

Running in parallel to HR 2847 was HR 870 [currently HR 1000], with the latter based on a Legal Authorization, on the books [15 USC § 3101], to maintain our unemployment, in America, at 3%, or less.

And asserted, here, is that this Legal Authorization is being ignored [and we have 12 million jobless in America]--as a direct result of the above *belief*—and our expectation that the Market will fix our unemployment crisis.

Unemployment is a "social" problem, with serious social consequences [we, as a society, have the responsibility to solve]--but even setting this aside--We are asking the Market to solve a problem it is *incapable* of solving.

The solution proposed, here, is the NEIGHBOR-TO-NEIGHBOR JOB CREATION ACT: A federally mandated, Social Insurance, owned by our employed—to provide a fund to hire/train our unemployed. For a modest policy cost of 4% of salary we can create more "private-sector" jobs in 6 months, than our current path in 6 years.

Essential in implementation.

1] It must be based on the premise that we have far more work that needs to be done in America—than we have persons to fill these jobs—[the notion that we would need "make work" jobs—is both a myth, and patently absurd]!

2] It must have renewable funding. This is NOT a "jump start" solution [such as HR 2847—HIRE Act]—i.e., funded until, in theory, the market will provide all the jobs we need [a fairy tale, at best, in any event]—

3] It will not add a dime to our deficit! Our unemployment is not the result of a lack of jobs, or money—but rather a lack of imagination—

See: FULL EMPLOYMENT IS A PRO-MARKET CONCEPT, Amazon

Jim Green, Democrat opponent to Lamar Smith, 2000

CHAPTER SEVEN

President Obama/Council of Economic Advisers:

86% of Americans believe that "anybody willing to work should be able to find a job".

Our true unemployment rate in America, however, is 12.3%.

To solve the problem of high unemployment--First we must make it a priority—and the sad truth is that we currently do not have ANY program SPECIFIC to ending unemployment!

Rather, our job creation is based on Republican "magical thinking"—i.e., we depend on jobs being created as a PRODUCT of something else happening—in this case, the success of the market—and if the market fails, the jobless are out of luck!

The incongruity in this mind-set is that the success of the market depends on people buying the products manufactured for the market to sell…and people don't buy the products of the market, if they are unemployed…[it is, in large part, the reason manufacturing has gone into the toilet, in America].

And unfortunately, most people have been led to believe that "the market can provide anybody wanting a job, with a job"—and most are unaware that "High and persistent unemployment has pervaded almost every OECD country since the mid-1970's" [i.e., it is disingenuous to say the market can provide everybody wanting a job, with a job].

The oxymoron to this day is: The belief that the market needs cheap labor to be used and discarded "at will", to increase profits—VS--people cannot afford to buy the products provided by the market--if they are unemployed.

In short, pervasive unemployment results in a social, economic, and political loss—even disregarding the devastating personal loss to the individual, and their families.

Extending unemployment benefits is necessary, but a stop-gap solution….What we need are programs

SPECIFIC to ending unemployment, we need to address it as a STAND-ALONE problem—a "social" problem we as a society must solve--and not condition our job creation on ANY other factor, or result.

For example, A Pro-Market solution--15 USC § 3101, which provides us with the "legal authorization" to limit our unemployment to "3%", and implementation of HR 870, or The Neighbor-To-Neighbor Job Creation Act.

See: FULL EMPLOYMENT IS A PRO-MARKET CONCEPT, on Amazon/Kindle

The definition of Full Employment is: Enough jobs available to meet the demand for employment by the available labor force.

Jim Green, Democrat opponent to Lamar Smith, Congress, 2000

CHAPTER EIGHT

President Obama/Council of Economic Advisors:

The electorate is awash in ignorance about how our economy works—and it has resulted in our having a House filled with lunatics! Isn't there some uncomplicated way we can educate the public, so that we have an informed electorate? The following letter to the editor has a Democrat slant—I am a Democrat—but the fundamentals are non-partisan:

Letter to the editor:

THE notion that the deficit should be put in the same category as the family budget—is patently absurd!

On the other hand—driving up our deficit to pay for an unwarranted war—such as Iraq, or drive up our deficit to line the pockets of the 1%--pander to GREED at the expense of the 99% [Supply-Side—the Republican One and Only Program—to this day]--is equally absurd!

We can't siphon America's wealth away from the consuming middle—without sending our economy into meltdown—as occurred under the Supply-Side scheme in 1987 and 2008—and collectively costing the taxpayers trillions in deficit spending to clean up their mess!

These are wastes of our deficit!

But were it not for the "government" using OUR tax dollars as a tool in our economic system—capitalism would collapse in a New York Second!

So there is good deficit, and there is bad deficit—ideally, the government wouldn't need this tool—but absent this tool we would have lost WW II!

When it is essential to use because the economy is in a sluggish recovery—such as now---it is good deficit—good for capitalism, et al--

The correct way to measure our deficit is as a percent of our GDP—and at present it is the lowest it has been since Clinton was president--

So why have the Republicans in Congress—particularly in the House, i.e., Ryan et al—suddenly gotten religion about our deficit?

Ryan was praising deficit spending as "deficits don't matter" when he voted to increase it by $7 trillion under Bush—but is now wailing about the evil of the deficit— HYPOCRISY just isn't a big enough word, here!

The Republican obstructionism, today, raises several questions: Are they using the American people as a battering ram [gutting Food Stamps as just one example]—to undermine President Obama?

Or are they just plain ignorant about how our economy works? Better yet, why do we hold back—the Democrats are in a dog fight, with a junk yard dog—the Republicans, today, are just NOT DECENT PEOPLE.....decent people don't act that way....

Either way, do yourself a favor and VOTE DEMOCRAT!

Jim Green, Democrat opponent to Lamar Smith, 2000
Bio info: http://www.amazon.com/James-L.-Jim-Green/e/B001KHZIMM/ref-ntt_dp_epwbk_0

CHAPTER NINE

President Obama/Council of Economic Advisers:

A German-national advised—in response to a question perplexing me for years—"Why on earth did the German people, with their rich cultural history, fall under the spell of a monster like Hitler"? He immediately responded "Because he put them to work".

There is a message in there of vital importance. The value humans place on being a productive member of society— the value we place on "work"—even raising the question if it should become a Human Right?

And while giving lip service to the plight of the unemployed--our market economies, the OECD, which includes the U.S., all suffer from high unemployment— and none address unemployment as a "social" problem— with serious social consequences--WE, as a society have the RESPONSIBILITY to address—Rather they leave the creation of employment up to the whims of the market-- And if the market fails, the unemployed are out of luck!

Which raises the question. The market suffers when people are unemployed—and the unemployed suffer when they are not working—so WHY on earth do our market-driven economies continue down such an unrewarding--a lose-lose path—where the market loses, and the unemployed lose?

The late Peter Drucker advocated for CEO salaries being limited to 20 times that of the lowest paid employee [the Swiss recently had on the ballot 12 times]—but it is argued that a brain-drain would occur if we didn't leave this to the market to set CEO salaries—

And whether or not this is true—WHY on earth do we persist in the anachronistic BELIEF that the market can provide anybody wanting a job, with a job [untrue since the mid-1970's]--particularly, and given automation, alone--an expanding and contracting public workforce is an INDISPENSABLE component to the EFFECTIVE functioning of a modern market economy?

Another factor, never discussed, is that the Market is as erratic as a runaway roller coaster...we can count on one hand the number of corporations, out of thousands—who have survived the past 100 years—employment is an everyday thing…FDR's Secretary of Commerce, Harry Hopkins now famous line "….people eat everyday" applies….i.e., Employment requires a steady hand--so why on Earth would we look to anything as unstable as the market to address? Or worse….as we do now, look to the market as our *sole* source of jobs? That is just plain nuts!

Indeed, in the U.S. we have the "legal authority" on the books [15 USC § 3101], to limit our unemployment to 3%--in short, at no time should our unemployment exceed 3%--So why does Washington avoid this legal authority as if it were the plague—such as indifference to deficit—neutral solutions, i.e., HR 1000, or via Social Insurance in The Neighbor-To-Neighbor Job Creation Act?

Please see: WHY WE CAN'T FIX UNEMPLOYMENT, Amazon

Highest regards,

Jim Green, Democrat opponent to Lamar Smith, Congress, 2000

CHAPTER TEN

President Obama/Council of Economic Advisers:

TO solve our unemployment crisis, as we advance into the 21st Century—WE MUST create a "reservoir of public employees"—as authorized in the "legal authorization" in 15 USC § 3101--with renewable funding paramount in our solution [i.e., we must abandon our "jump-start" mind-set].

It is a "win-win" solution—the jobless win, and the market wins!

At present, All of the OECD countries suffer from chronic high unemployment—and all are using the same methodology to create jobs:

They stand on one foot and then the other waiting on the market to create their jobs—

That is, job creation is intrinsically linked to the state of the market, and if the market fails—the unemployed are out of luck....

Unemployment is a "social" problem, with serious social consequences—but rather than being treated as a problem we as a society have the responsibility to solve—such as the cure for AIDS, or Polio—

Rather, we use a model making the solution contingent on an outside factor: The highly erratic nature of the market—with the empirical evidence, alone, offering consummate proof that we are on the wrong track—i.e., it will be 2017 before we return to even an anemic 5.5% jobless rate!

In short, we do not have on the table, at present, ANY program specific to addressing/ending this extremely serious social problem—and we need to ask WHY?

Further, the problem is compounded by work being lost to "automation"—but rather than turning back the clock, we need to apply the maxim—We need to adapt and change in a world that is changing whether we like it or not....

Specifically, going forward we need to acknowledge that an expanding and contracting public workforce is an INDISPENSABLE component to the EFFECTIVE functioning of a modern market economy.

And in the absence of this truism, at present, both the jobless, AND the market suffers!

IT IS IMPOSSIBLE TO BE A CHRISTIAN, AND VOTE REPUBLICAN, Amazon/Kindle

Jim Green, Democrat candidate for Congress, District 21, TX, 2000 www.Inclusivism.org jgreen5@satx.rr.com

CHAPTER ELEVEN

President Obama/Council of Economic Advisers:

As a market-driven, "free-enterprise" system, It is of critical importance to limit our unemployment to 3%, or less. At a 3% unemployment rate we reach the threshold point above which unemployment starts undermining the Market.

Further, the harm to a robust and vibrant market economy increases exponentially with each percentage point increase in our unemployment rate [i.e., the coefficient of variation--high unemployment/sluggish recovery is not a non-sequitur, and evident by our stagnant April 2014, Jobs report of 6.7%].

Every year approximately 4 million children are born in America, 2.5 million Americans die—and weighing in other factors, conservative estimates predict that, at present, we need, to create just over a million jobs a year to keep up with the population.

The problem with our anemic job creation, in America, is endemic to our current system—and based on antiquated and erroneous economic theory: 1] Fix the market, and this will in turn fix unemployment---and, 2] The market can provide anybody wanting a job, with a job—the first doesn't work, the second isn't true.

In the mid-1970's the world economy underwent a major paradigm shift resulting in "High and persistent unemployment pervading almost every OECD country since the mid-1970's.", according to Dr. William F. Mitchell, as well as every credible economist—and to this day, double digit unemployment is ubiquitous in the Eurozone.

Economists disagree over what caused this paradigm shift—proposed here is a single word… "modernity"—the colliding forces of automation, globalization, technology, etc., reached a critical mass in the mid-1970's—rendering the Market incapable of creating the jobs necessary to the demand—and with "automation", alone, this will be even more and more true as we advance into the 21st Century.

Unemployment is a "social" problem, with severe consequences--We, the larger society have the responsibility to address—and in 1978 the U.S. responded directly to the above paradigm shift in the economy, AND the dire social consequences of unemployment—a PRO-MARKET solution WE HAVE INEXPLICABLEY YET TO IMPLEMENT [15 USC § 3101]—and it provides us with the "legal authorization" to end our unemployment crisis tomorrow!

In closing, a few profound words by President Obama, while on a trip to Sweden.

"There no contradiction between making public investments and being a firm believer in free markets."

He went on to expand "Sweden also has been able to have a robust market economy while recognizing that there are some investments in education or infrastructure or research that are important…".

Please see: FULL EMPLOYMENT IS A PRO-MARKET CONCEPT, on Amazon/Kindle

Jim Green, Democrat opponent to Lamar Smith, Congress, 2000

CHAPTER TWELVE

President Obama/Council of Economic Advisers:

Since the Great Depression, economic consensus has advocated as the means to turnaround an economy in meltdown, is via fiscal policy which employs deficit spending—most recently in 1987 and 2008, and as advocated by Keynes, in the 1930's.

And this model was employed, with particular vigor, in the economic collapse of 2008-9—with our U.S National Debt now in excess of $17 trillion, and counting.

But we have another way to get there that is: 10 cents on the dollar being added to our deficit, that is Pro-Market [what we are doing now is Anti-Market], and is deficit-neutral in ending our unemployment crisis. It is defined as Economic Inclusivism – www.Inclusivism.org .

It is made up of the following components:

1] We would enforce the "legal authorization" in Public Law 15 USC § 3101, so that at no time would our unemployment exceed 3%. This is a Pro-Market solution. The market thrives when we have a robust, employed, consuming workforce—and this would also stimulate manufacturing—both manufacturing and the market are hampered with high unemployment.

2] We would employ The Buffer Stock Employment Model, advocated by Dr. William F. Mitchell, Australia. An expanding and contracting public workforce—that expands during downturns in the market, and contracts as employees return to the private sector [and triggered at 3% unemployment]. Further, this acknowledges that, given automation, alone, an expanding and contracting public workforce is an *indispensable* component to the *effectifve* functioning of a modern market economy, with this dilemma exacerbated in our 21st Century economy.

3] We would employ the deficit-neutral model for job creation advocated in HR 1000, or deficit-neutral--The Neighbor-To-Neighbor Job Creation Act.

> A federally mandated, Social Insurance, owned by our employed to provide a fund to hire/train our unemployed. For a modest 4% of salary policy cost we can create more "private-sector" jobs in 6

months, than our current path [HR 2847], in 6 years. Further, this has strong political support-- 86% of Americans believe that "anybody wanting to work should be able to find a job....".

In short, we would both eliminate the serious "social" consequences resulting from unemployment, as well as replace the current practice of adding to the deficit to stimulate the economy.

See also: FULL EMPLOYMENT IS A PRO-MARKET CONCEPT, on Amazon/Kindle

Highest regards,

Jim Green, Democrat opponent to Lamar Smith, Congress, 2000

CHAPTER THIRTEEN

President Obama/Council of Economic Advisers:

Low unemployment is smart business—the market thrives when we have a robust, employed, consuming workforce—and low unemployment is essential in creating a decent and civilized society—unemployment is a "social" problem—we, as a society, have the responsibility to address....

And we have the "legal authorization" [15 USC § 3101], on the books, to limit our unemployment to 3% in America, tomorrow--i.e., at no time should our unemployment rate in America exceed 3%....

In short, there is NO upside to unemployment—the jobless lose, and the market loses....high unemployment/sluggish recovery is not a non-sequitur....

SO WHY, when we have the means to solve the most pernicious social/economic problem facing America, today—do our "policy makers" run from this solution like it were the plague? World travel was out of the question when consensus had it that the world was flat....i.e., where is our national dialogue so the American people can participate in the solution?

86% of Americans believe that "anybody wanting to work should be able to find a job"—our "legal authorization" has solid political support....

The answers, here, would appear to put to an acid-test the recent studies: If we are a democracy, or an oligarchy, in America...and the most baneful belief in America, today, is: "The market can provide anybody wanting a job, with a job"—all of the data tells us this belief is FALSE.....

This also raises the question: Why are we afraid to take this next step in our social evolution? Why do we run from an obvious, and legal means, to bring about a solution?

And, HR 1000/The Neighbor-To-Neighbor Job Creation Act [NTN] are deficit-neutral—we have far more work that needs to be done in America, than persons to fill these jobs—[we have 8,800 pending infrastructure jobs, alone] so it is not the lack of jobs, or money that is standing in the way....

SO WHY are these questions not front center—and being given ONLY the highest priority in Washington? And rather than "fix the market, and this will in turn fix unemployment" [our current, and highly ineffective path to recovery], not being replaced with "fix unemployment, and this will fix the market" [the path we should be on]?

It is the silence that justifies asking these questions.

FULL EMPLOYMENT IS A PRO-MARKET CONCEPT, Amazon/Kindle

Jim Green, Democrat opponent to Lamar Smith, District 21, TX, 2000

CHAPTER FOURTEEN

To the Editor: The NEW YORKER

ECONOMIC INCLUSIVISM: A Pro-Market Solution For Our Unemployment Crisis [what we are doing now is Anti-Employment, and Anti-Market]

Pope Francis has presented us with a challenge for social and economic justice—but until we get honest about the "Belief" that is preventing us from moving into our 21st Century economy...here and throughout the OECD [the market-driven economies, including the U.S.]--both the jobless and the market will suffer.

During the 2008 election the electorate spoke loud and clear—*Fix Unemployment* With majorities in both the Senate and House, I thought the Democrats would employ Public Law 15 USC § 3101, which provided them with the "Legal Authorization" to limit our unemployment to "3%". In short, at no time should our unemployment in America exceed "3%".

To my dismay—the Democrats opted for 1950's economic theory, with employment now being restored at a snail's pace, and the result has been a disaster [I believe the 2010 election was retaliation for not fixing unemployment, and also ushered in a House full of lunatics]1

The Democrats would have had broad public support in 2010 with 3% unemployment, and now that is in jeopardy for 10 years, and it left us with a Washington in paralysis.

Also, according to the CBO, on our current path, it will be 2017 for us to get back to even an anemic 5.5%, with unemployment benefits long since expired—[the House Republicans are threatening not to renew the current rollover, as I write]--and if the market fails, the jobless are out of luck....

The puzzlement for me is why would our brightest and best make such a critical error? The solution to a problem is measured by results—and the data, alone, shows this result to be miserable.

Further, this is not limited to our leaders in America—and is also true throughout the OECD, with Eurozone 12.1%, as I write, and 25% in Greece and Spain, common. I would add that I believe all of these leaders are genuinely concerned with fixing joblessness.

So, I ask, why do our leaders keep applying 1950's economic theory, in a 21st Century economy—particularly, given the most serious social problem facing us today, widespread unemployment?

And my take is because it is based on a pervasive, but false, "Belief":

THE "BELIEF/MYTH" THAT THE MARKET CAN PROVIDE ANYBODY WANTING A JOB, WITH A JOB —[and our market economies stand on one foot and then the other waiting on the market to solve a problem it is INCAPABLE of solving--more on this shortly—this "Belief" is bedrock for Republicans(1), and let's not forget that pervasive belief once had it that the world was flat]….

And thus the policies and laws to solve unemployment, in our market-driven economies, have been framed around, and based on this "Belief"....and it cannot be disregarded, what psychologists call "groupness"—a circle the wagons mind-set by vested interests to preserve the status quo—for instance by President Obama's Council of Economic Advisers, and their counterparts in the OECD.

Also, many in the "rank and file" have so bought into the myth that ONLY the market can create jobs—they have joined with the 1% who deny climate change to justify drilling the Rockies down to an anthill---to assure their having a job—the planet be dam--ed!]....

But, this hasn't been true since the mid-1970's, and "High and persistent unemployment has pervaded almost every OECD country since the mid-1970's", according to Dr. William F. Mitchell, and every credible economist [and pervasive unemployment dominates our news programs daily].

What happened in the mid-1970's, as the result of a Grotian Moment-like paradigm shift in the world economy, is open to debate—I believe it was the result of the converging forces of automation, globalization, technology, etc., reaching a critical mass in the mid-1970's—i.e., we became victims of our success, and since, we have celebrated automation in the workplace, and then got a "deer in the headlights" regarding the displaced employee [a problem which left uncorrected, will grow exponentially as we advance into the 21st Century]. In the U.S. we defined the impact of this economic shift as "malaise".

A factor apparently not considered throughout the OECD is that unemployment is a "social" problem, with serious social consequences—We, as societies, have the responsibility to solve….and when every waking moment in capitalism is spent pondering how to eliminate as many of us humans, as possible, from the workplace—to increase profits—why on earth would we turn to the market to solve a social problem--that is antithetical to its objective?

In sum, the world has changed, our solution for unemployment hasn't, and the result has been a disaster—i.e., as a result of the "Belief", above-- nowhere in the OECD do we have ANY program SPECIFIC to ending unemployment!

Rather, our job creation is based on Republican "magical thinking"—i.e., we depend on jobs being created as a

PRODUCT of something else happening—in this case, the success of the market—and, as noted, if the market fails, the jobless are out of luck!

And to illustrate just how far off base we are: We currently have a program--ostensibly to provide employment for seniors seeking some extra bucks to off-set the high cost of living—but rather than providing a job—the objective is to train seniors for a job in the Market—with training they don't need, and at 80, WHAT JOB? It is disingenuous for this program to hold out the offer of employment for seniors!

For perspective on the stubborn and sub-conscious nature of this "Belief" [3% is perceived as unsustainable, for example], ask: Why can we land on the Moon, but we can't fix unemployment? And why would we turn to anything as erratic as the market for a solution? And why do we ignore data which clearly tells us we are on the wrong path?

My solution is The Neighbor-To-Neighbor Job Creation Act [hereafter NTN]: A federally mandated, Social Insurance, owned by our employed, to provide a fund to hire/train our unemployed. For a modest 4% of salary policy cost we can create more "private-sector" jobs in 6 months, than our current path [HR 2847], in 6 years. Further, this has strong political support--86% of Americans believe that "anybody willing to work should be able to find a job...." [a quote from President Obama in "The Audacity of Hope"].

The market thrives when we have a robust, employed, consuming workforce--high unemployment/sluggish recovery is not a non sequitur. NTN is a "win-win" solution—The unemployed win, and the market wins.

Jim Green, Democrat candidate for Congress, 2000
www.Inclusivism.org jgreen5@satx.rr.com

(1) The Republican's job creation theory [asserted by Republicans as if it were fact] is cut taxes for the 1%, they will build factories with the windfall of cash—and we will all have a job in the corporation—it is BS—been there, did that—[Reaganomics] it has a 7 year shelf-life before the economy collapses [1987 & 2008], it drove us into a $10 trillion hole to dig out of, it cost the taxpayers $6 trillion more [and counting] to clean up their mess, and a 14.4 million job loss—In short, rather than being

pro-market [which they boast] the Republican agenda is a MENACE to the market! And the "Belief", above, explains why Republicans spew out broad-brush, mean-spirited, irrational blather "The jobless are lazy", etc., etc.....

The lesson from Supply-Side is that we cannot siphon America's wealth away from the consuming middle, without sending our economy into meltdown [and yet, it is the Republican *One and Only* program, to this day]! And, the Republican/Conservative propaganda that the government is an intrusive problem "and private enterprise a reliable solution" is both archaic and destructive in a 21st Century economy.

A BRIEF ADDENDUM. If one concludes that the market cannot provide everybody wanting a job, with a job—then they must look elsewhere to solve the problem of unemployment—and this, I believe, is the perceived conundrum faced by those charged with fixing our unemployment crisis—their *ONLY* choice is "public-sector" jobs, and many fear this will compete with "private-sector" jobs—but this is specious--for one, the employees are doing different things—and in the trade-off there is a far greater loss to the market by not employing an expanding and contracting public workforce [Buffer Stock Employment Model--Dr. William F. Mitchell, Australia]--that expands during downturns in the market and contracts as employees return to the private sector—[triggered at 3% under Humphrey-Hawkins].

And apparently least understood is that this is an INDISPENSABLE, *a sine quo non* component to the EFFECTIVE functioning of a modern market economy. Humphrey-Hawkins is Pro-Market—and they had it on the nose in limiting our unemployment to 3%.

And as just one illustration—were it not for the moneys from Social Security Insurance [Social Insurance] in the U.S. percolating up through our economy during the 2008 meltdown, we would not be talking about having narrowly averted another Great Depression, we would be buried in one! A weapon, incidentally, available to President Obama, that was not available to FDR—and it also explains, in large part, why we have not had a Great Depression since.

And, perhaps it needs to be added that Social Insurance is democracy in its highest form. Cicero [106-43 BC] and reiterated by Christ "The people's good is the highest law"—and American citizens pooling their money for the common good—is DEMOCRACY, in fact--[some confused Republicans/Conservatives think the will of the American people is socialism, communism, or like blather, and evident by the current war against democracy by the Republicans in Congress—[i.e., the Republican's war against the will of the American people on gun control, as just one example]!

On a societal level, our choices are: Adapt and change in a world that is changing whether we like it or not—or create a Police State to hold anachronistic [unworkable] solutions in place….and in America, we have, sadly, opted for the latter….

Three vital components in creating a buffer stock of employees, include: 1] it would be based on the premise that we have far more work that needs to be done, than persons to fill these jobs ["make-work" jobs, is archaic thinking]. 2] It must have renewable funding [this is not a "jump-start" solution, as currently practiced], and 3] it will not add a dime to our deficit.

Finally, the notion that this would result in massive federal job creation is absurd, archaic—and HR 870 provides the correct model, with grants to local jurisdictions—and our local unemployment offices become employment offices.

To overcome this "Belief" we need to think differently, for instance, our mind-set should change from fix the market, and this will in turn fix unemployment—to fix unemployment, and this will fix the market. And our current anemic result in job creation is consummate proof of the fallacy that "market-only" solutions work [Ron Paul, et al]--it is a fallacy.

At present, American law still has one foot on the plantation--American "employees" are seen as "A Pool Of Slaves" [persons without rights—a slave by definition], to be used and discarded "at will"—

While conversely, the human need to be a productive member of society cannot be stressed strongly enough (2), and in time, in America, it will be looked upon as a Human Right—after all, our "economies" are only about one species—us—us human beings--it is one of the few things communism got right. If it isn't clear yet, I am a capitalist....I staunchly support: Make a better widget, sell it for a million bucks, and retire in South Florida—but the truth is, labels have become a menace and our political parties need to evolve into a single label, objective: "eclectic problem-solver"....[and a fitting label for President Obama—but undermined by our current political paralysis].

(2) Our current indifference to this human need is the reason for our epidemic of workplace violence, a pernicious incarceration rate, and our youth shooting each other at an alarming rate in every major city in America—and at the core of this indifference, and a plethora of other ills--is an anachronistic "BELIEF"....

Bio Info: http://www.amazon.com/James-L.-Jim-Green/e/B001KHZIMM/ref=ntt_dp_epwbk_0

See also: FULL EMPLOYMENT IS A PRO-MARKET CONCEPT, and ECONOMIC INCLUSIVISM: NEO-CAPITALISM Inclusive Pro-Market Solutions For Our Social Problems, on Amazon/Kindle

CHAPTER FIFTEEN

President Obama/Council of Economic Advisers:

Every time a person becomes unemployed, it cuts into corporate profits....but this is not on the table....and when we multiply this by 11 million, in the aggregate it is an extremely serious problem for corporate America, regarding the bottom line....

Better yet, WHY is this not on the table?

When we speak of our jobless, we speak of their plight—and that is in no sense diminished by our looking at the other side of this equation—

Unemployment is a "social" problem, with oft dire social consequences, we as a society have the responsibility to address.

To get the oligarchy/plutocracy on board, however, we need to change the dialogue—we need to change the message TO: The loss in corporate profits resulting from unemployment—which, given automation, alone, grows exponentially as we advance into the 21st Century.

> "3% is the zero-sum threshold above which unemployment starts substantially undermining the Market--and the loss in income to the Market is compounded exponentially with each percentage point of increase in unemployment, above 3%".

Currently, many in the oligarchy/plutocracy still have one foot on the plantation, cling to the erroneous belief that they need "a pool of slaves" to be used and discarded "at will" [the current status of employment law in America—which they wrote]—and promote the pernicious lie that "The market can provide that the market can provide anybody wanting a job, with a job"---but this mind-set is cutting off their nose to spite their face in the process—

Thus, how do we change the dialogue—how do we build consensus to repair our unemployment crisis?

Consider the following analogy.

30 years ago gays getting married was on no one's radar—it simply wasn't discussed. Perhaps it started with

a single couple who saw this as a right—but in the years since the consensus grew and currently the majority of Americans believe gays should have the right to marry.

And the point is that the same dynamic could be applied in our economic evolution re the unemployed.

The bottom line is, Humphrey-Hawkins [15 USC § 3101] was ahead of its time—when it was signed into law in 1978, by President Carter—Now it is Indispensable to the Effective functioning of our 21st Century market economy....

And, the over-arching point is that until we change the dialogue--change the message--we are not going to solve our insidious unemployment crisis in America.

FULL EMPLOYMENT IS A PRO-MARKET CONCEPT, Amazon

Jim Green, Democrat opponent to Lamar Smith, Congress, 2000

CHAPTER SIXTEEN

President Obama/Council of Economic Advisers:

RE: LAYING the FOUNDATION for RECOVERY &
GROWTH

President Obama had a weapon in addressing our
economic meltdown in 2008, in America—not available
to FDR during the Great Depression:

And this was the billions from Military Retirement and
Social Security Insurance percolating up through our
economy—

In short, were it not for these moneys we would not be
talking about having narrowly averted another Great
Depression—we would be buried in one!

Also, this model is a "win-win"—it addresses a critical
social need, as well as benefits the economy i.e., the
market—and yet the Republicans want to tamper with
this vibrant social benefit in their short-sighted agenda to

pander to the GREED of the 1%--it is their One and Only program!

In short, this model is a "pro-market" concept—and least understood. An INDISPENSABLE component to the proper functioning of the market going forward in the 21st Century—

The market thrives when we have a robust, employed, consuming workforce—but given the proliferating volatile nature of the market [the obsolete cycle is getting shorter and shorter], *the market is no longer capable of producing the jobs necessary to its viability*—and it is essential that we address this void with public sector jobs—ON BEHALF OF THE MARKET!

> The Buffer Stock Employment Model--an expanding and contracting public workforce—that expands during downturns in the market, and contracts as employees return to the private-sector—[in theory, triggered under Public Law 15 USC § 3101, anytime our jobless rate rises above 3%] was introduced at the University of Chicago in 1998, by Dr. William Mitchell, signaled a solution to this economic dilemma facing a modern market

economy. Fix the market and this will fix our unemployment crisis vs fix unemployment and this will in turn fix the market—[

"Conventional Wisdom", to date, has exclusively taken the former path—and the result has been a disaster—and in spite of a 6.3% unemployment rate—we still have 12 million jobless Americans, a sluggish recovery—and a CBO projection of 5 years just to get back to 5.5%--with unemployment benefits long since expired!

Proposed, here, is The Neighbor-To-Neighbor Job Creation Act: A federally mandated mutual insurance, owned by our employed, to provide a fund to hire/train our unemployed. For a modest policy cost of 4% of salary we can reduce our unemployment to 3%, within a year of passage, and as "authorized" under Public Law 15 USC § 3101. The lone legislation in Washington, at present, relevant to the above is HR 1000 [currently in Committee].

See also, "OUR GREED AND IGNORANCE" on Amazon/Kindle; www.Inclusivism.org .

Jim Green, Democrat candidate for Congress, 2000

CHAPTER SEVENTEEN

June 6, 2013

F. Michael Kelleher,
Special Assistant to the President
Director of Presidential Correspondence

President Obama/Council of Economic Advisers:

We are obsessed with the index provided by GDP—is it up, is it down—to measure the health of the economy—but have no such "alarm" index when it comes to unemployment….

For instance, the definition of "Full Employment" is all over the map among economists—from zero [Job Guarantee] to 9%--with the former based on anybody willing to work, should be guaranteed a job….

But ignored, at present, is that FULL EMPLOYMENT IS A PRO-MARKET CONCEPT—and thus an index regarding unemployment to measure the health of an economy is equally as important as GDP.

And while our number crunchers will hang on every digit, with the release of the Labor Department's May Jobs Report June 7, 2013—the fact is, the health of our economy is measured by a tread down....rather than an index that sets off alarms anytime our joblessness exceeds 3% [we have the legal authority to limit our unemployment to 3%, but inexplicably ignore this law!].

Our economy is only about ONE species...us, us human beings...any yet our economy does not factor in the HUMAN RIGHT to be a productive human being—and thus we, as a society, have an obligation to step in to address this HUMAN RIGHT.

We have an index to measure the status of our economy by how much stock we have left in our warehouses....etc.,.....

And, our economic lexicon should include, for instance, an index such as PALR [Percent Above Legal Right]—or PAL for short, that would tag the percent our unemployment is over 3%--for instance, at 7.5%--our PAL Index would be 2.5, or two and one-half times over what is should be in a healthy economy.

Most importantly, this would bring unemployment front and center in a measure of the health of our economy—rather, than it being a step-child—and our policies would change to:

Fix unemployment, and this will fix the market—rather than the other way around---i.e., the failed path we are on now that will take until 2017, per the CBO, to get back to even an anemic 5.5% unemployment rate—and our unemployment benefits long since expired!

In short, the path we are on now is ANTI-MARKET, while claiming to be pro-market, our current policies actually HARM OUR ECONOMY!

See Also: ECONOMIC INCLUSIVISM, on Amazon/Kindle

Jim Green, Democrat opponent to Lamar Smith for Congress, 2000

CHAPTER EIGHTEEN

RE: September 2013 Jobs Report:

President Obama/Council of Economic Advisers/Fellow Democrats:

OUR RECOVERY INCHES ALONG DRAGGING A SACRED COW:

"Most [Americans think] that anybody willing to work should be able to find a job....". Indeed, a Zogby Poll found that 86% of Americans think this.

AND, we have the LEGAL AUTHORITY, on the books, to make this a reality in Public Law 15 USC § 3101—a deficit-neutral, Pro-Market means to address the wishes of the American people [see below]....

So why do we have 11.3 million unemployed Americans, and a 7.3% unemployment rate [quadruple for minority youth]?

We are a democracy…under our Constitution the government serves at the will of the American people….

Under the Public Law, above, there is no time in which our unemployment rate in America should exceed 3%….

SO WHAT IS CAUSING THIS CHASM BETWEEN PUBLIC WILL, AND POLICY IN WASHINGTON?

And, virtually every policy maker in Washington must share the blame by default….

In looking for a solution to our unemployment crisis in America, they almost universally default to the anachronistic and totally unworkable belief in a modern market economy—a SACRED COW:

THE BELIEF that the market can provide everyone wanting a job, with a job [and if the market fails, the unemployed are out of luck]….

And yet, the market has been less and less capable of creating enough jobs—given automation, technology, globalization, etc., since the mid-1970's—with pervasive high and persistent unemployment in most of the OECD countries since that time...

It appears, our policy makers celebrate automation and then get "a deer in the headlights" regarding the displaced worker—and the adverse "social" consequences of unemployment.

As a result our policies have been framed around. Fix the market, and this will fix unemployment—when our framework should be exactly the opposite. Fix unemployment, and this will fix the market.

FIXING UNEMPLOYMENT IS ANTITHETICAL TO THE OBJECTIVE OF THE MARKET—IT ISN'T WHAT THEY DO.....

Proposed, here, is deficit-neutral/Pro-Market THE NEIGHBOR-TO-NEIGHBOR JOB CREATION ACT. A federally mandated Social Insurance, owned by our employed, to provide a fund to hire/train our unemployed. For a modest 4% of salary policy cost we can reduce our unemployment to 3% within a year—and this will create more "private-sector" jobs in 6 months, than our current path [HR 2847] in 6 years.

HR 1000/FULL EMPLOYMENT IS A PRO-MARKET
CONCEPT/ IT IS IMPOSSIBLE TO BE A CHRISTIAN, AND
VOTE REPUBLICAN Amazon/Kindle

Jim Green, Democrat opponent to Lamar Smith, Congress,
2000

CHAPTER NINETEEN

President Obama/Council of Economic Advisers:

Capitalism is ideal in producing and selling corn flakes and cars—It doesn't work in solving "social problems" such as unemployment and our healthcare....

And when we have tried "privatization" to solve our social problems—it has been a disaster:

Essential programs have been cut—such as the elimination of text books from the Job Corps education program—to increase profits, and cronyism has been rampant—

And in our "for profit" healthcare system, billions of dollars are siphoned away from the premiums we send in—and do not go to the healthcare of ANYONE—but rather is used to pay for lobbyists, to make the CEO's filthy rich—and spent on propaganda ads to keep it that way!

Further, it attracts a few who see healthcare as a means to get rich, rather than cure the ill....

The truth is, we currently have a blended system—and they are, in fact, indispensable to each other:

Were it not for Social Security Insurance moneys percolating up through our economy in 2008—we would not be talking about having narrowly averted another Great Depression—We would be buried in one!

Social Insurance is a vital ingredient in building a vibrant and decent society—And, invent a better widget, sell the company for a million bucks, and retire in South Florida [capitalism]—is as well a vital ingredient in building a vibrant and decent society.

So why do we have this war of words pitting the two against each other—rather than educating the American people regarding the indispensable symbiotic relationship they have to each other?

Most Republicans ask God in their prayers at night to be protected from becoming communists, or socialists, or even worse "liberals"—

And this war of words disguises that the Republican Party, today, is not the Pro-Market party they boast—but rather their policies are, in fact, Anti-Market—destructive to capitalism!

Pandering to the GREED of their wealthiest contributors—the Republican One and Only program—is NOT a Pro-Market concept!

Another misnomer in the war of words, is right-wing invented "entitlement"—a word that should be banned from honest discussion—do we refer to our auto insurance as an "entitlement"?

And when Social Security Insurance brings in more that it pays out, i.e., is deficit-neutral--how is that an "entitlement", and why is it portrayed in our graphs as a "government expense"—or even included in these graphs? If a corporation reported a massive loss on a product they in fact made money—they would be charged with fraud in a New York Minute!

The list goes on—please see: OUR GREED AND IGNORANCE, on Amazon/Kindle

Jim Green, Democrat congressional opponent to Lamar Smith, 2000

CHAPTER TWENTY

FAIL-SAFE ELECTRONIC VOTING

TO THE READER: Given you have gotten this far, and
agree with the proposed changes—and particularly given
the pernicious Citizens United—our democracy, and the
above, or any, progress, will be in peril absent a "fail-safe"
electronic voting system. The following is my proposed
solution, and like every solution proposed, here, feed-
back--your proposed improvement, etc. is welcomed.

THE FAIL-SAFE ELECTRONIC VOTING ACT

1) EVERY electronic voting machine (hereafter EVM),
must be inexpensive, identical throughout the U.S. in a
1/150 ratio, and *must count and produce a hard-copy of
the recorded votes.* In addition, an extra copy of their
recorded votes would be produced (not necessarily a
hard-copy), marked "Voter's Copy", and containing
"NOTICE: Do Not Destroy Until Every Election On Your
Ballot Is Certified". [If Wal-Mart handed us a piece of
paper with the words "trust us" as a receipt for our

purchases—we would be outraged—and yet, this is our current electronic voting nightmare—but in this case it is our democracy at risk]!

2) *After confirming that their votes are recorded correctly,* the voter would then insert the hard-copy ballot into a software-free (count only) optical scanner (hereafter OS), for a second count. The hard-copy ballot would be retained by election officials in the event a candidate asks for a recount (*not possible under the current system, and which undermines the legality of each such election)*. The EVM and the OS must be manufactured by different companies (which is universally true today).

3) Election officials assigned to oversee the EVM, would be prevented by law from overseeing the OS, and vice-versa, and stiff criminal penalties would be imposed for violations.

4) Further, every EVM would be programmed with raw data re the total registration rolls, by party, and norms for their voting history, etc.,----as an "alert" to a possible irregularity, such as an "under-vote"—or "vote-flipping" etc., and *standards* established to suspend certification

where there is an "improbable result", at least temporarily, of a particular election until the discrepancy is cleared up. (This is what computers do best, and it would be very easy to create such a program).

5) At the end of the election day, tallies would be taken from the EVM and the OS, for each candidate. *If the tallies didn't balance for any given election, or if there is an "alert", that election cannot be certified until the "error" is corrected.* If the candidates agree (the victory is certain), minor discrepancies in the count could be disregarded. While probably rare, the Voter, or a random sample of Voters, would be required by law to return their Copy of the recorded votes to the election office to clear up any "error", or where an "alert" signals the need for same.

6) Further, every state provides for a recount when the total vote falls below a certain percent of difference between the candidates, impossible to conduct with the current EVM. And thus Congress must mandate the following regarding presidential candidates: A RUN-OFF election is mandated and triggered in those states where the percent of total vote is less than .5% of difference between the two candidates; said election to be held on the second Saturday following the election, on PAPER

BALLOTS ONLY, and contain ONLY the names of the relevant candidates, for instance: "Barack Obama, Democrat" and "John McCain, Republican"—with oversight in counting by a representative(s) of each party—said procedure providing more than adequate time to meet the Electoral College mandate [Ideally, all of this could be eliminated if we did away with the Electoral College, but until then....]. NOTE: Had this been the law in 2000, Al Gore would be our president, and America would have been spared the economic, etc., disaster that followed!

7) Finally, absent the above safeguards, and until these safeguards are in place--Congress must mandate that PAPER BALLOTS, ONLY, can be used in our presidential elections. This is not a "partisan" issue, it is a "pro-democracy" issue. Most importantly, this will return the responsibility for our elections, and our vote counting, back into the hands of the individual voter, where it belongs, and out of the hands of "corporate control"---*it is after all "our democracy", itself, that is at risk if we don't take these steps---and in that regard, is there any time or cost differential that is too great?*

Jim Green

CHAPTER TWENTY-ONE

I didn't write the following. It is a cut and paste from FACEBOOK, or some blog [would like to give credit if knew the author]--but it is so on target regarding how "fear" is driving Conservative policy in America today— i.e., is undermining America and our progress—and relegating America to a Third World country status, rather than a world leader—FDR had it on the nose in "All we have to fear, is fear itself"…at his inaugural in 1933….

"Conservatives are such cowards: they are afraid of gay people getting married or serving in the military; they are afraid of bringing terrorists to super max prisons in the US from which no one has ever escaped; they are afraid of the boy scouts letting gay kids in; they are afraid of everyone voting and are constantly suppressing the vote under some bogus voter fraud theory; they are afraid of letting students vote at their universities; they are afraid of women having the right to choose; they even are afraid of women getting contraception [the real issue actually is a women's agency and control over their bodies]; they are afraid of immigration reform leading to citizenship because they are afraid of-- name whatever reason; they are afraid of mandating gun purchasers to undergo background checks for crazy people and terrorists; they are afraid of people smoking pot; they are afraid of climate change being real and contradicting their beloved Bible; they are afraid of legitimate campaign reform; they are afraid of Muslims; they are afraid of blacks; they are afraid of atheists; they are afraid of hippies; they are afraid of socialists; they are probably still afraid of monsters under their beds; they are just rank cowards and keep making things up to be afraid of."

CHAPTER TWENTY-TWO

[I couldn't resist including this...and yes I am the author.....]

A MESSAGE FROM GOD

MANY CENTURIES AGO, a man of the cloth, we don't know his name, and in a flash of insight (perhaps induced by peyote) told his flock that "sex is a sin". And lo and behold he learned that by taking a very natural and healthy part of our life and turning it into something that was "dirty and nasty", that he could imprison his flock, and fill his coffers, and hallelujah it was a great day for the Lord!

Quickly, his miracle spread to other churches in his village, and then to the next village, and then the next county, and then state, and soon it spread to all the churches in the ancient world, and all of their flocks cowed in fear and shame and became imprisoned, and their coffers over-floweth. Hallelujah, it was a great day for the Lord!

And to keep the myth alive they started inventing stories, half-baked stories, that made no sense to anyone who is rational, such as "Mary was a virgin"—well, she just had to be a virgin because she would never partake in anything that was dirty and nasty, like sex (if you're doing it right), and this was necessary to make "sex is a sin" make sense...so they invented a Mary that was "sinless"-- you get the picture. And their coffers over-floweth. Hallelujah, it was a great day for the Lord!

No one seemed to be bothered that when we play tricks on the human mind by taking something that is very natural and healthy, such as sex, and make it dirty and nasty that all kinds of bad things happen to the human mind.

Such as most pedophiles, and most serial killers, and voting Republican, and unwarranted suicides, and most mental illness, and unwanted pregnancies. (Teens not wanting to have sex is the perversion, not the other way around, and by replacing sex education and condoms, with unrealistic "abstinence", and by using blather about "low self-esteem" to shame them into not "sinning"—We have a teen pregnancy in the U.S. twice that of England and Canada!).

But none of this mattered, because their coffers over-floweth, and Hallelujah, it is a great day for the Lord!

There is a cure--------Tell these right-wing loonies to shove it....

GOD

ABOUT THE AUTHOR. I was employed in our Criminal Justice System for a cumulative 20 years as a probation officer, with 5 of those years as a chief probation officer. I authored the concept of "Shock Incarceration" which became law in Kansas in 1970, and then was adopted in numerous jurisdictions in the U.S. and also spread to Europe—it is currently identified in the U.S. as "Boot Camp" [as the means to "shock" the young offender—and a total distortion of my original intent—like many ideas, once released, they take on a life of their own]. I also instigated establishment of the first Court Psychiatric Clinic in the U.S., in conjunction with psychiatrists from the Menninger Foundation, as a chief probation officer. Finally, I was the Democrat candidate for Congress, District 21, TX, 2000. I would most define myself as a Social Ecologist-- [albeit my degree is in Psychology]. My web page is www.Inclusivism.org –which has been on the internet since 1996.

A BRIEF ADDENDUM: When the U.S. Supreme Court denied certiorari—where the violation of my constitutional rights were obvious, and criminal negligence on the part of the government defendants in the death of our son, equally obvious—[detailed in THE HARVARD BOYS CLUB, Amazon/Kindle]--I filed a Petition for Rehearing [which is automatic]—and included the following. The Clerk of the U.S. Supreme Court called me at my work in California, and asked that I withdraw the "cartoon" [a reprint from The NEW YORKER] from my Petition. I refused on the basis of the First Amendment, and it remains in the archives at the U.S. Supreme Court [Docket #: 79-1627], to this day. The wording [not that clear] is: "Excellent, excellent. A fine blend of truths, half-truths, and blatant falsehoods".

IN THE

Supreme Court of the United States

October Term, 1979

No. 79-1627

JAMES L. GREEN,

Petitioner,

VS.

"Excellent, excellent. A fine blend of truths, half-truths, and blatant falsehoods."

OTHER BOOKS BY THIS AUTHOR ON
AMAZON/KINDLE/BN:

- THE HARVARD BOYS CLUB: Hitler's Assault On Our Freedoms From His Grave
- MY LETTERS TO PRESIDENT OBAMA: Confessions Of A Compulsive Letter Writer
- OUR GREED AND IGNORANCE: Poses A Far Greater Threat To America, Than Terrorism
- LETTERS ON STEROIDS: Confessions Of A Compulsive Letter-To-The-Editor Writer
- THE FIRST TIME I HAD SEX: And, The Religious Intolerance Attack On America
- WHY PRESIDENT OBAMA LOST THE 2012 ELECTION: A Wake-Up Call
- ECONOMIC INCLUSIVISM: Neo-Capitalism/An Anthology: Inclusive pro-market solutions to our social problems
- AMERICA IS ONE SICK MF: Why Greed-Driven America Went Off The Rails….
- EVERY GIVEN SUNDAY: A Scientific Formula To Predict NFL Games

- IT IS IMPOSSIBLE TO BE A CHRISTIAN, AND VOTE REPUBLICAN

And others: http://www.amazon.com/James-L.-Jim-Green/e/B001KHZIMM/ref-ntt_dp_epwbk_0

-

www.ingramcontent.com/pod-product-compliance
Lightning Source LLC
Chambersburg PA
CBHW051337170526
45166CB00002B/853